The World of Mythology:
Indian Mythology

By Jim Ollhoff

VISIT US AT
WWW.ABDOPUBLISHING.COM

Published by ABDO Publishing Company, 8000 West 78th Street, Suite 310, Edina, MN 55439. Copyright ©2012 by Abdo Consulting Group, Inc. International copyrights reserved in all countries. No part of this book may be reproduced in any form without written permission from the publisher. ABDO & Daughters™ is a trademark and logo of ABDO Publishing Company.

Printed in the United States of America, North Mankato, Minnesota.
012011
092011

Editor: John Hamilton
Graphic Design: Sue Hamilton
Cover Design: Neil Klinepier
Cover Photo: Gonzalo Ordóñez
Interior Photos and Illustrations: Alamy-24 & 28; AP-pg 11; Corbis-pgs 7, 17, 19, 21, 22, 23, 26, 27, 28 & 29; Getty Images-pgs 11 & 18; Glow Images-pgs 20 & 25; Granger Collection-pg 13; Himalayan Academy Publications-pg 9; Thinkstock-top/bottom border image and pgs 5, 8, 10, 13, 14, 15, 16 & 32.

Library of Congress Cataloging-in-Publication Data

Ollhoff, Jim, 1959-
  Indian mythology / Jim Ollhoff.
    p. cm. -- (The world of mythology)
  ISBN 978-1-61714-722-7
  1. Mythology, Indic--Juvenile literature. 2. India--Religion--Juvenile literature. 3. Hinduism--Juvenile literature. I. Title.
  BL2001.3.O55 2011
  398.20954--dc22
                        2010041628

CONTENTS

THE MIGHTY MYTH

What do Ulysses, King Arthur, Luke Skywalker, and Jake Sully (the hero of the movie *Avatar*) have in common? All four of these characters star in a heroic journey. It is a classic kind of story, or myth, that is told by almost every culture on Earth.

Similar themes appear in myths all over the world. Most myths contain gods and goddesses. They often have great powers. They also usually have a glaring weakness. Most mythologies contain heroes who try to do great things. Sometimes the heroes are human. Other times they are gods. Sometimes they even are half-human and half-god.

Most mythologies also include a cast of characters called archetypes. They appear over and over in many stories. Tricksters are a kind of archetype. They are rule-breakers who fool people. Some tricksters are evil, while others just want to have fun.

In Indian mythology, some gods come to Earth in the form of people, animals, or even other gods. These forms are called avatars. It's the same god, but in a different physical form. The 2009 film *Avatar* borrows this idea by telling the story of Jake Sully, a man who uses an avatar on an alien planet. The avatar is Jake, but in another physical form.

Most stories and myths have similar plots and characters. Some psychologists say this comes from the needs of the human mind. Since we are all human, with the same basic needs, it's no surprise that myths have many things in common worldwide. It pays to understand our myths so that we can understand ourselves.

Above: Ganesha, the Indian god of success and good luck. India's culture includes beliefs and customs from many parts of the world.

THE HISTORY OF INDIA

People have lived in India almost as long as humans have been on Earth. The first organized civilization in the land may have risen about 2600 BC. Located near the Indus River (now in Pakistan), this culture created cities and was home to tens of thousands of people.

About 1500 BC, a people called Indo-Iranians invaded. Coming down from the northwest, they took over the land. India absorbed the new people. India has what is called an "assimilative culture." The culture includes beliefs and customs from many parts of the world.

The country was conquered by the Greek king Alexander the Great in 327–326 BC. However, his army couldn't hold the country for very long. A local chieftain named Chandragupta Maurya defeated Alexander's troops and founded the first great empire. This Mauryan Empire lasted about 150 years. Other kings and empires ruled the land in the following centuries, but the people of India always relished the idea of many ideas, many stories, and many myths.

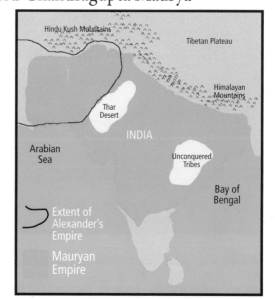

Right: A map of the Mauryan Empire.

Above: The Greek king Alexander the Great invaded and conquered part of India.

However, his troops could not hold the country for very long.

THE SOUL OF INDIA

The mythology of India is incredibly rich and varied. Myths were very important to the people of India. While Westerners might look to their history to learn who they were, the people of India looked to their myths. Mythology played a role in almost everything. Down through the centuries, the stories were told, retold, reinvented, and connected to other stories.

Older beliefs in India are sometimes called the Vedic traditions. They are named after religious writings called the Vedas. Many of these beliefs were rituals to sacrifice animals so that the gods would do what the people wanted. Between 800 and 500 BC, new scriptures emerged. These were called the Upanishads. The Upanishads didn't replace the Vedas. They just added more ideas. It was out of this mix of beliefs that Hinduism arose.

Right: The Hindu god Indra was the supreme god of the Vedic traditions. Indra was the god of war and weather. He was said to be able to send rain and thunderbolts at his choosing. A rainbow was said to be a sign of his presence.

In Hinduism, a person's soul never dies. It is reborn into a new life form.

One of the ideas of Hinduism is reincarnation. According to this belief, the souls of dead people go into a newly born life form. If a dead person spent his or her life being kind and loyal, then the soul goes into the baby of a higher-class person. If the person was a criminal, their soul might go into the body of a reptile. People hope that they can live so well that they advance through higher forms and get out of the endless cycle of reincarnation. Then they can join with the Brahman, the divine force of the universe.

Above: A man works in a field in India. Dharma means to do your job as well as possible, whatever that job may be. Dharma was meant to bring order to the world, but it often reinforced placing people in castes.

In order to live well and come back in a higher form, people must perform their spiritual duty, or their dharma. Dharma means to do your job as well as possible, whether you're a butcher, baker, candlestick maker, a parent, or a child. Dharma brings spiritual order to the universe.

Dharma often reinforced the caste system in India. Castes are classes of people. In a caste system, higher castes are well respected, while lower castes are often discriminated against. Even in modern India, the caste system is often recognized, usually in rural areas.

Above: A Dalit, or Untouchable, man repairs shoes on the street. As a member of India's lowest caste, he barely makes a living. *Left:* Today, as they have for many years, people protest and fight against India's unfair caste system.

At the top of the Indian caste system were priests, the most respected and honored. Rulers and warriors were next. Beneath them were professionals and merchants. Finally, at the bottom, were common laborers who performed menial tasks. (This is where we get our word *outcast*). Usually, it was forbidden to marry someone not in your caste.

Indian mythology has a seemingly endless number of gods and heroes. In Western cultures, most people like their heroes to be good, and their villains to be bad. But in India, many of the gods and heroes do both good and bad things. Many of the most feared gods also fight off monsters and demons. Indian mythology is complicated, but it is very rich and deep, with many different kinds of stories.

BRAHMA THE CREATOR

Brahma is the Hindu creator god. He was born in a lotus flower, which was in the navel of the god Vishnu. He spent most of his time meditating. Out of his meditation came the different parts of the universe.

Brahma is often pictured with four or five heads, so that he can see everything. In some versions of the myths, he created all of the other gods. He was the father of the first human, named Manu.

As Indian mythology grew, Brahma became less popular. He was less involved in people's lives. People began to tell more stories of other gods like Vishnu and Shiva, who were more exciting and personal.

The priests who served the god Brahma were called Brahmins (sometimes spelled Brahmans). Sometimes Brahma is confused with the word Brahman. Brahman is not a god. It is the soul of the universe, the force of life.

Right: An image of Brahma, the Hindu creator god.

Above: The Hindu creator god Brahma is often pictured with four or five heads, so that he can see everything.

VISHNU THE PRESERVER

The god Vishnu was a kindly god. He was always interested in preserving and protecting people. Before Brahma created the universe, Vishnu leapt three times to mark the boundaries of the universe. He also held up the pillar that separates heaven from Earth, so that heaven didn't come crashing down.

Vishnu appeared on Earth in many forms, called avatars. Some traditions say he had 10 avatars. Other myths say he had more. But whenever the world was threatened, one of Vishnu's avatars came to fight for humanity or give guidance.

Vishnu in his boar avatar form.

One of Vishnu's avatars was a fish who warned Manu (the first man) of a coming flood. Another avatar was named Varaha, who was a giant boar. When a demon stole the Vedic scriptures and then pushed the Earth into an ocean, it was Varaha who rescued the Earth and got the scriptures back.

Above: Vishnu in his first avatar form as a fish. Some traditions say he had a total of 10 avatar forms.

SHIVA THE DESTROYER

Shiva was the fearsome destroyer, punishing the wicked as well as sometimes destroying the entire Earth. He was often pictured dancing, with many arms. He had a third eye on his forehead that erupted in flames. He was sometimes pictured with a pale face and a blue neck, because he drank poison that would have killed humanity.

Shiva was a complicated god. He lived with demons, but he was merciful. He was violent, yet he protected the weak. He destroyed, but he was thoughtful about it. He destroyed so that something new could be created, similar to the way an acorn must be destroyed to make an oak tree.

In one story, Brahma and Vishnu were arguing about which one of them was the greatest. Then Shiva appeared as a giant flaming pillar between them. Brahma tried to fly to the top of the pillar, but it was too high. Vishnu dug down to try to find the bottom of the pillar, but it was too deep. Both Brahma and Vishnu were forced to admit that Shiva was the most powerful.

Above: Shiva was a fearsome destroyer. He was sometimes shown erupting in flames.

KALI THE DEMON KILLER

One of the most fearsome gods in Indian mythology was Kali. She killed demons, but sometimes became so frenzied that she also destroyed the world. Kali was often pictured with long fangs, a blood-red tongue, and a necklace of human skulls.

In one version of Kali's birth, she was born when the goddess Durga was fighting a terrible, powerful demon. This demon could reproduce himself with a single drop of his own blood. Kali burst out of the forehead of Durga, and then killed the terrible demon. Kali then quickly drank all the blood of the demon so that none of it could fall to Earth and create more demons.

There were professional assassins and criminals in ancient India who killed in the name of Kali. In the language Hindustani, they were known as "sthaga," or thieves. British officials in the 1800s called them thugees. That is where we get our word for a violent person—a thug.

Right: Indian criminals sometimes killed in the name of Kali. They were called "sthaga," which became the English word for thug.

Above: Kali is an Indian goddess who killed demons, but also could destroy the world.

INDIAN CREATION STORIES

Most cultures have several creation stories. India probably has more creation stories than any other culture. In one Indian creation story, a giant egg floated on the ocean. Brahma cracked it, and out of the egg came mountains, rivers, the sky, and everything else. There were many versions of this myth, some involving Vishnu, others involving Shiva.

Another creation myth had Vishnu lying on the back of a giant serpent. A lotus flower—a symbol of peace—grew from Vishnu's belly. Inside the lotus flower was Brahma, who emerged from the flower and then created the universe.

A much earlier version of the creation story involved a god named Visvakarman. There was nothing but chaos, but Visvakarman began to churn the chaos, in the same way a farmer might churn milk to make butter. Soon, out of the chaos the world was created.

Right: Vishnu lies on the back of a giant serpent.

Above: A painting shows the churning of the sea of milk.

POPULAR INDIAN GODDESSES

The gods and goddesses of India were powerful and intelligent. Many sought to promote peace and do away with evil.

Saraswati: Sometimes called the mother of the universe, she was the wife of the creator Brahma. In one tale, Brahma created her himself. In another version, she was the daughter of Shiva and Durga. She gave the world Sanskrit, the language of the Hindu scriptures. She was the patron goddess of learning, wisdom, and the arts.

Right: Saraswati, the wife of the creator Brahma, was the goddess of learning, wisdom, and the arts.

Above: Durga, a powerful goddess born in flames, slays the buffalo demon.

Durga: She was a very powerful goddess. When Vishnu and Shiva were fighting the powerful buffalo demon, they shot flames from their mouths. Durga was born in these flames, capturing and then killing the buffalo demon. In some versions of the myth, she was married to Shiva, and so she helped to rid the world of demons. Shiva's masculinity and Durga's femininity represent a balance to the universe. Durga is fierce, with vampire-like teeth. But she also was the goddess of creativity and the patron deity of sleep, and she gave yoga to the world.

Right: The god Vishnu rides with his two wives: Bhudevi the Earth goddess (left) and Lakshmi the goddess of good luck and wealth (right).

Bhudevi: Probably an ancient mother Earth goddess, she was added to the mythology of India. She helped create the universe. In some versions of the myth, she was married to Vishnu. Like Vishnu, she had many forms and avatars.

Lakshmi: This goddess of good luck and fortune was a wife of Vishnu. She was the perfect beauty, born as an adult from the waves of the ocean.

Ushas: The goddess of the dawn was reborn every morning. She was the daughter of the sky and the sister of the night, and she rode a chariot across the sky each morning.

Sati: One of the older gods in India was Daksha, and Sati was his daughter. Sati married Shiva, even though Daksha disapproved. Daksha and Shiva fought until Shiva cut off Daksha's head. Shiva then put a goat head on his father-in-law's shoulders. Sati threw herself into the fire in protest, but came back to life as the goddess Parvati.

POPULAR INDIAN GODS

Indra: One of the earliest gods in India, Indra was considered the king of the gods. He was a god of storms and was a great warrior. As Vishnu and other gods became more popular, a story emerged that Vishnu lifted a mountain with his finger to shield the Earth from Indra's torrential storms. Over time, Indra was demoted to a less-important rain god.

Ganesha: This god was the patron deity of success and good luck. Originally, he was the son of Shiva and Parvati. Parvarti, the mother, told Ganesha to guard the door while she bathed. However, Ganesha took her words too seriously, and wouldn't even let his father Shiva enter the bath. Shiva angrily cut off his son's head. Understandably, Parvati was outraged. So Shiva took the first head he could find and put it on Ganesha. It was an elephant head, and so Ganesha was pictured as an elephant-headed man.

Left: Ganesha, the elephant-headed god of good luck, pictured with his parents Shiva and Parvati.

Krishna: One of the avatars of Vishnu, Krishna was himself also worshiped as a god. Krishna battled demons, including his evil uncle. He was quite popular and had more than 16,000 wives. Krishna was accidentally killed by a hunter, who shot an arrow into Krishna's foot.

Surya: The god of the sun was Surya. In some myths, he was an avatar of Vishnu or Shiva. He was often pictured sitting in front of the sun, sometimes with three eyes and four arms. He rode a chariot across the sky each day.

Rama: Rama was one of the most popular avatars of Vishnu. Rama was probably based on a much older series of myths about Indra, one of the earliest Indian gods. As various demons and monsters were destroying the countryside, Rama used Shiva's bow, which no human had ever been able to use, to rescue the people.

GLOSSARY

ARCHETYPE

A character that appears over and over in myths or stories.

AVATAR

A different physical form taken on by a god.

BRAHMAN

Not a god, but the soul of the universe; the force of life.

BRAHMINS

The priests of the god Brahma.

CASTES

Classes of people. Some castes were more respected than others.

DALIT

The lowest class of people in the Indian caste system. Also known as Untouchables.

DHARMA

One's spiritual duty.

HINDUISM

A religion of India.

KING ARTHUR

A warrior king of the British castle-city of Camelot. King Arthur may, or may not, have been real. British stories tell of King Arthur and his Knights of the Round Table, who brought peace to the land.

LUKE SKYWALKER

A fictional heroic character from the *Star Wars* movies.

MEDITATE

To think deeply about a subject, usually while relaxed and calm.

PATRON DEITY

A protector or guardian god.

SACRIFICE

The act of killing an animal or human as an offering to a god or gods.

ULYSSES

A king, hero, and adventurer of Roman mythology. Also known as Odysseus in Greek mythology.

UPANISHADS

Scriptures of India, emerging later than the Vedas.

VEDAS

Early scriptures of India.

INDEX

DyAnne DiSalvo

A Castle on Viola Street

HarperCollins*Publishers*

*T*o my great-uncle Charlie 02/02/02 (1902, that is)

"All deuces, baby."

The author would like to acknowledge the following for their help with her book:
William Menke, Habitat for Humanity International
Doug Wagner, Metro Camden Habitat, New Jersey
The "Monday crew" at Sacred Heart of Camden, New Jersey

The art is done in gouache, colored pencil, and china marker.

Library of Congress Cataloging-in-Publication Data
DiSalvo, DyAnne.
A castle on Viola Street / by DyAnne DiSalvo.
p.   cm.
Summary: A hardworking family gets their own house at last by joining a community
program that restores old houses.
ISBN 0-688-17690-9 — 0-688-17691-7 (lib. bdg.)
[1. Dwellings—Fiction.]   I. Title.
PZ7.D6224 Cas   2001   00-40889
[E]—dc21   CIP
AC

Typography by Stephanie Bart-Horvath
1   2   3   4   5   6   7   8   9   10
❖
First Edition

ABOUT HOUSING ORGANIZATIONS

While helping to build a house, a young woman said to me, "My family has a home; we just need a house to put it in!" Not long after that, a group of volunteers got together and helped her family build a simple, decent house where they could put their home.

About one billion people in the world today don't have a safe or affordable place to live. Some have lost their homes to natural disasters. Many live on small fixed incomes or may not make enough money to afford to rent or buy a house. Many people, including those in religious organizations, governments, corporations, and nonprofit organizations, are working hard to make this better.

In more than two thousand communities around the world, people who feel strongly about the need for housing have formed Habitat for Humanity affiliates. Affiliates are groups that bring together volunteers and resources to build simple houses. Habitat for Humanity homeowners pay for their houses in part with three hundred to five hundred hours of what is called "sweat equity." This means they must help build other people's houses as well as their own and also do other work with the affiliate.

Habitat for Humanity International, Christmas in April, World Vision, and the Local Initiatives Support Corporation are just a few of the organizations working to build houses and help communities develop the resources they need for success.

—Millard Fuller
Founder and President,
Habitat for Humanity International
Americus, Georgia

In the old days, before I was ten, we rented an apartment on Emerald Street. It was a small place to live in for one whole family, but somehow we made the room.

There always seemed to be enough to go around, even with five people at our table.

Every morning my father would get up even before the sun. "Someday things will change around here," he would whisper to me. He usually said this during the winter when the house was beginning to feel chilly. Then he'd kiss us good-bye, tuck up our blankets, and leave for his job at the diner.

My mother worked part-time in the downtown bakery while my sisters and I were at school. After school she'd sit on the stoop and watch us play.

Sometimes my mother would flip through a magazine. She'd show me pictures of houses with gardens and porches. They all looked like castles to me. I'd puff out my cheeks when I looked at our place. It was old and peeling and sorry.

That's when my mother would hug me and say, "Our family is rich in more ways than we can count."

On Saturday mornings my mother would weigh my pockets down with quarters for the Laundromat.

"Hold Andy's hand," she'd tell my sister.

Then my mother would slip two brown-bagged lunches in the wagon with a dollar for a treat. My sister and I would bump our cart to the Soap & Go on Viola Street.

Now, across the street from the Soap & Go were three boarded-up houses. My father said it was a shame. "Somebody should do something about that," he'd say whenever he saw them. So when a truck pulled up and workers unloaded equipment, I started to pay attention.

"What's going on over there?" a lady at the Soap & Go asked.

Mr. Rivera pointed to a flier that was posted up front.

"I'll bet it has something to do with this," he told her. The flier had a picture of a house and said YOU TOO CAN OWN A HOME.

After our laundry was dried and folded, I took my sister by the hand and rushed our wagon back to Emerald Street.

At supper I told my parents all about what I had heard and seen. My father scrambled eggs with extra zest, and my mother put ice in our water.

"There's a meeting tonight," I said. "Seven o'clock at the school."

Later on, when my parents came home, they were just as excited as I was.

"This organization buys empty houses and fixes them up like new!" said my mother.

"And if you're interested in helping to fix up a house for other people," my father continued, "then one day other people will help fix up a house for you."

That sounded like a good plan to me. It would be nice to live in a house that wasn't so chilly in winter.

"So we signed up," my father told me. "Can we count on you to help?"

I hugged them so tight I almost fell out of bed. I think they knew my answer.

Well, you know how sometimes, when you never believe that anything will ever be different, then one morning you just wake up and nothing is the same? That's what happened to our family that spring when the project on Viola Street began.

Clang! Bang! Bang! Smash! Those workers started early.

"Take a good look," my mother told us. "That's what we'll be doing soon."

"Are all those people getting a house?" I asked.

"Some of them will," my mother said. "But anyone who wants to can help. It's called volunteering."

Piece by piece, the inside of the first house came apart—one old bathtub, some cabinets, sinks. Slats of wood and piping piled up like a mountain full of junk in the Dumpster.

Most people on the block were happy about the project, but other people were not. The lady next door said, "No banging before nine o'clock!" Some people laughed and said out loud, "Who would want a house in a neighborhood like this?"

But my father would smile and whisper to me, "Sometimes new things are hard to get used to and people are slow to change."

On the weekends, when our family showed up, a leader
called out the assignments.

"Everyone here will have a special job to do," she said.

My mother scraped wallpaper off crusty walls that
crumbled like toast. My father and I worked together. He lifted up
old linoleum tiles by sliding a cat-hammer underneath. My job was to
carefully hammer down nails on the floorboards when he was through.

Some volunteers, like us, hoped to have a house one day.

"We're looking forward to living in a place without broken windows and leaky pipes," Mr. and Mrs. Rivera said.

My father said he couldn't wait to have a house that would have heat all winter.

My sisters were still too young to help with all the construction. But my mother told them, "Being little is no excuse not to pitch in." She had them squeeze juice from bags of lemons to make fresh lemonade. Then they took turns pouring and passing the cups all around.

At the end of the day there was always a lot of sweeping to do.

"I've never seen so much dust in my life," Mrs. Tran said, covering her nose.

My mother held a dustpan while I pushed the broom. My sisters giggled whenever they saw me wearing my safety mask.

On Saturday nights I'd be so tired, I'd practically fall asleep right after supper.

"You're doing good work," my father would say. And he'd thank me for helping our family. He'd say, "Big dreams are built little by little, and we are making a start."

In those four months I learned a lot about putting things together. Once I even found a piece of wood that my father said I could keep. I thought that maybe I could use it to make something on my own.

One day Mr. Tran gave everyone some news. The new house would be theirs!

"Everything is beautiful," Mrs. Tran said. She stood smiling inside the framed front door. She watched her daughter paint the big front room. The kitchen had shiny linoleum floors and brand-new appliances. There even was a washing machine! Upstairs was a bathroom and three carpeted bedrooms. Out back there was a place for a garden.

When the Tran family moved in, they threw a potluck supper. My father and I took care to make something extra special that night.

"Since I've been promoted to cook, I like to whip up a storm," he said.

We not only celebrated the Tran family's being the owners of their new home, but we also celebrated because we knew we were one house closer to our dream.

Things were really changing on Viola Street now. "This neighborhood looks like it's shaping up," the lady at the Soap & Go said. Volunteers were working on two more empty houses. And of course the Trans next door didn't mind when we wanted to get to work early.

This fall our family was notified that we'd be working on our own house next spring—number one-forty-six Viola Street. Whenever we pass it, my mother says, "I can imagine it finished already." I've already got my bedroom picked out. It's the one with the window by the yard.

During the winter, I made a birdhouse from my piece of wood and gave it to my mother. My mother was more than pleased about that. She said, thanks to me, now even the birds would have a nice little place to call home.

I used to dream that we had a million dollars to buy a house of our own. But in real life all it cost us was a lot of hard work. Anyway, it seems to me like all the money in the world couldn't buy us what we have now on Viola Street. It's just as my father says: Big dreams are built little by little, and we have made a start.